Saving the Planet, one da...

In this short guide, you wi... an do which will make the wo...

These mostly apply to people living in industrialised countries.

The kindness quotient will go sky high and climate change will be significantly reduced.

The first 5 are big ones that will take time to achieve, but the rest are simple steps that we can all take every day. The impact will only be apparent if a significant proportion of the 7,000,000,000 + people currently alive take this on board.

Headline Change-makers

These are explained and expanded upon in the following pages. To get your attention, here they are presented as simple statements.
In no particular order:

- Stop eating meat. If that's too much avoid beef and live on chicken and bacon.

- Drive an electric car.

- Make sure your house is properly insulated.

1

➢ Make it clear to every politician that opposing nuclear missiles is the only policy that will guarantee your vote and that not opposing them will mean that you will not vote for them.

➢ Every time you have to make a decision which will impact on another person or sentient animal, make sure you make the Kind choice.

And that's it. Job done.

➢ **Stop eating meat. If that's too much avoid beef and live on chicken and bacon.**

➢

Using good agricultural land to feed cattle is chronically inefficient.

If all the acreage was used to grow food for people, hunger could be eradicated.

Cows produce vast amounts of methane. Bad.

Eating RED MEAT is one of the top 10 causes of preventable cancer.

Not convinced? OK just cut down if you can't cut out. I live on fruit, fish and vegetables Monday to Thursday because I am weak. The other three days I'll eat what I like except that I've bought some smaller plates so they look full and I eat less.

I will eat the occasional steak if I'm out and not feel guilty but I am moving as quickly as I can towards eating no red meat at all.

> **Drive an electric car.**

You only have to walk alongside a busy main road to completely understand the problem presented by cars and lorries. The noxious fumes they pump out are poisoning all of us and our children and our planet.
I recently returned from Beijing where the problem is so acute that people wear masks and it feels as if your throat has been sand-papered all the time.
Electric cars deal with all of this so long as the power they run on is created in a clean way. It doesn't help if the

electricity is made by coal fuelled or Nuclear power stations.

When returning from Xian to Shanghai our train {electric} flew by a coal power station, which we could make out through the smog on a sunny day. Ironically, behind it were 3 wind turbines swirling the muck around as they spun.

The level of development of a civilisation is measured by how many steps there are between the energy it uses and the natural sources of the Sun and Gravity. Wind farms, tidal generators and solar roadways are definitely the way forward and you, whenever you get a chance to vote, should consider each parties view on this as a priority.

> **Make sure your house is properly insulated.**

When you walk around wherever you live on a cold winters day, how many houses do you see with no frost on the roof? Make sure that your house isn't one on them and get it properly insulated.
Making energy to power our increasingly technology dependent world is THE BIG PROBLEM. Insulating your house properly is one of the easy ways you can reduce your consumption. If we all do it, the need to make the energy in the first place is much reduced and the world will be a happier healthier place.
If you can't afford proper insulation you can achieve a lot with old carpets and discarded clothing laid out in the attic. Books you'll never read again can also be helpful.

➢ **Make it clear to every politician that opposing nuclear missiles is the only policy that will guarantee your vote and that not opposing them will mean that you will not vote for them.**

Nothing we try to do will be of any use if any of the world "Leaders" who have control of these monstrous devices decides to fire one off. Their selfish stupidity would undoubtedly trigger a cataclysmic exchange that would put an end to all of us, but not to them. We all know that no one intends to use them and that the whole thing is about making money but, tragically, whilst they are around the possibility of some crazed nutcase taking power and thinking it's OK exists. Look around at the current crop and ask yourself if you really trust them enough.

This is the argument:
If an enemy government fires its nuclear missiles at us we are all going to die, except those with access to deep bunkers and an early warning system.

Who are they?

They are the leaders, their family, friends and cronies whose mismanagement of world affairs caused the problem in the first place. That doesn't include you or me.

Since we are all going to die we have choices.

The first response of most people is to fire "our" missiles back at the "enemy".
But let's examine that.

If I handed you a 3-year-old child, a razor blade and a blow torch and said to you that I wanted you to skin it as it screamed, burn the raw flesh then stamp it to death you would think me mad and call the police, and quite rightly so.

If you support the possession of nuclear weapons, and therefore their potential use, that is exactly what you would be doing to the children of the nation that attacked us.

You would destroy their hospitals and their schools and their care homes and millions of people who bare you no ill will, will die in pain and torment as they hold their children in their arms.

In most cases these people, who would be brutally murdered with your consent, will have spent their lives being oppressed and dictated to by governments over which they have no control and which they did not choose.

The perpetrators of the attack on you and your loved ones would, undoubtedly, be in their deep shelters with years of food and oxygen and would be unharmed and your act of mass destruction would be completely futile.

It is not good enough to say that possession of these foul machines is a deterrent because, for the reasons above, no sane person could ever use them and no-one should, therefore, ever say that they would.

This is August 2017 and I am in the United Kingdom. Our Prime Minister and the Leader of our Official Opposition have both said that they would push the button and initiate the slaughter of the helpless millions. For that reason, I have dismissed the first and will never vote again for the second, and nor should you.

I am not a pacifist. I just require that our military response is targeted and effective.

Here's a better idea.

Build your submarines and missiles if you must, but fill the warheads with leaflets that say, in the appropriate language, something like this:

"Your leaders have murdered us. As you read this our cities are smoking ruins and our children lie dead in the arms of their slaughtered parents.
We have chosen not to respond with violence and terror. We give you the gift of life and so die with a clear conscience.
We ask you to use this gift well.
When your criminal leaders emerge from the deep bunkers in which they are now skulking, drag them from their palaces and show them no mercy. Do to them what they have done to us then hang their smoking carcases from lampposts and bridges.
Revenge us".

In this way, at least the right people would die.

➢ **Every time you have to make a decision which will impact on another person or sentient animal, make sure you make the Kind choice.**

➢

 Let's be clear. We are not actually talking about saving the planet. If we continue to get things wrong the planet will shrug us off. The ice caps will melt, sea levels will rise between 58 and 80 metres, civilisation in global terms will collapse and, eventually, the human race will die out. Then, in a millennium or two, the planet would recover and continue its journey without us.
We are talking about saving the human race. If we manage that there has to be a reason.

How much nicer would the world be if we all lived by the simple maxim above. 7,000,000,000 random acts of kindness every day, even if we only manage one each.

The rest of this book is devoted to suggesting things that you can do which don't involve demonstrating or protesting. Saving the Planet {I know, I just like the title} one step at a time. To get the full impact you have to image each one multiplied by the number above. They mostly apply to the lifestyles of those in the West, but many are truly universal. They are in no particular order and you don't have to do them all, just as many as you are comfortable with!

Number 6.

Every time you get in to your car. Settle yourself in, sort everything out and put your seat belt on BEFORE you start the engine.

That minutes' worth of emissions multiplied by a billion cars would make a huge difference.

Number 7.

In the winter turn your central heating down by 1 degree a day until someone notices. All that power you are wasting is made somewhere and the less we need to make, the better off the planet will be AND you save money.

Number 8.

Still on the heating theme. Before you turn on the heating in the first place, try wearing an extra layer of clothing.

Number 9.

If you don't really need to use the car, walk. Even 10 minutes a day of brisk walking counts as exercise. You'll get fitter, manage your weight better, save money and reduce pollution.

Number 10.

Holiday in your own country. Air travel is one of the biggest pollutants. Every air mile not flown will help. If you want to go abroad consider trains and ferries and explore Europe.

Number 11.

Always take your own bags when you go shopping. Plastic is in many ways wonderful but it's also a curse, particularly when it ends up in landfills or, even worse, the ocean.

Number 12.

Buy locally sourced food. Do you really want to eat food that has travelled half way across the world in huge ships that pump out pollution? Reduce those transport miles in every way you can.

Number 13.

Accelerate smoothly. That over-revving wears out the engine faster, burns oil, uses more petrol and, frankly, makes you look silly.

Number 14.

Brake gently. Tyres are a huge problem. The longer yours last, the less there will be that need to be disposed of.

Number 15.

If you are lucky enough to have a garden big enough, grow your own vegetables. Not only do they taste nicer, you will also get exercise and fresh air. Gardening is very therapeutic, it just makes you feel good AND it saves you money. If you over-produce, give it away to someone who will appreciate it.

Number 16.

Just finished a mug of tea or coffee? Give it a quick rinse and put it back in the cupboard. Over 12 months you will reduce the number of times you run the dishwasher by many times thereby saving money and reducing energy consumption. You can apply this to any item.

Number 17.

Do you really need to wash everything you wear when you've only worn it once? Try putting that tee shirt back on the hanger at least once. Imagine a billion washing machines each doing one less cycle a month.

Number 18.

Ignore sell by / use by dates. They lead to chronic waste and are mostly irrelevant. The manufacturers want you to throw stuff away so you buy more of the same. If it doesn't smell bad and it isn't slimy, you can almost certainly eat it. If in doubt throw it out, particularly when feeding children or the vulnerable, but otherwise, enjoy it!

Number 19.

Over filled kettles are killing the planet! Don't boil enough water for six cups when you only need one!

Number 20.

Be frugal in the bathroom. Turn the shower down by 1 degree a day until you notice. Put half the toothpaste you normally would on the brush and see if it works just as well. Similarly, reduce the amount of shaving gel, shampoo etc. Save money, reduce waste and take down energy consumption.

Number 21.

Is that jar REALLY empty? Or that tube or tub or whatever. Many containers seem to be designed to promote waste. Persevere and get the last morsel out. It may sound mean but you need to multiply what you do by everyone who uses that product and then you'll see the importance.

Number 22.

LED standby lights! Turn everything off at the plug. A billion households with half a dozen appliances on standby is a lot of power. TURN THEM OFF.

Number 23.

Recycle everything you can. Give things you don't need {as opposed to want} to charity shops or those who need it more than you. Landfills will be less full. Your house will be less cluttered and you will feel great about yourself.

Number 24.

One day each week behave as if electricity was never discovered. Rise with the sun, sleep at sunset. Walk in the daylight. Play together. Eat together. Eat salad and fruit, cheese, cold ham and tinned fish. Drink water, fruit juices or squash. All that power saved and an improved diet as well!

Make a perfect day.

Number 25.

When you have acted on each of the suggestions in this book. Recycle it. You are within the lifetime of people who routinely {2017} cut up their own toilet paper.

All images were sourced through www.creativecommons.org and should be free for use. If you own any of these and you would like them removed please leave a comment on Amazon.

Printed in Great Britain
by Amazon